BACK to BASICS

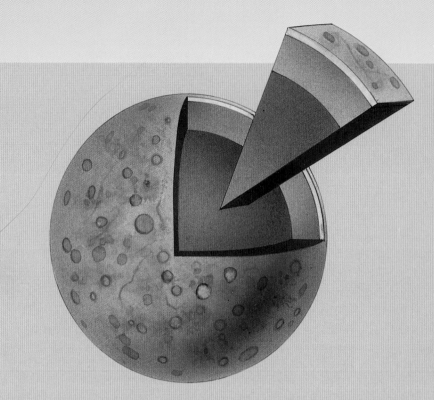

The Back to Basics series was devised and produced by McRae Books Srl, Borgo S. Croce, 8, Florence (Italy)

Publishers: Anne McRae and Marco Nardi
Text: Brian Williams, Vicky Egan
Editing: Vicky Egan (Starry Dog Books Ltd)
Main Illustrations: Fiammetta Dogi
Other Illustrations: Antonella Pastorelli, Studio Stalio (Alessandro Cantucci, Fabiano Fabbrucci,)
Design: Marco Nardi
Layout: Nick Leggett (Starry Dog Books Ltd)
Color separations: Fotolito Toscana, Firenze

© 2008 McRae Books Srl, Florence

CIP data available

Printed and bound in Malaysia

BACK TO BASICS

THE SOLAR SYSTEM

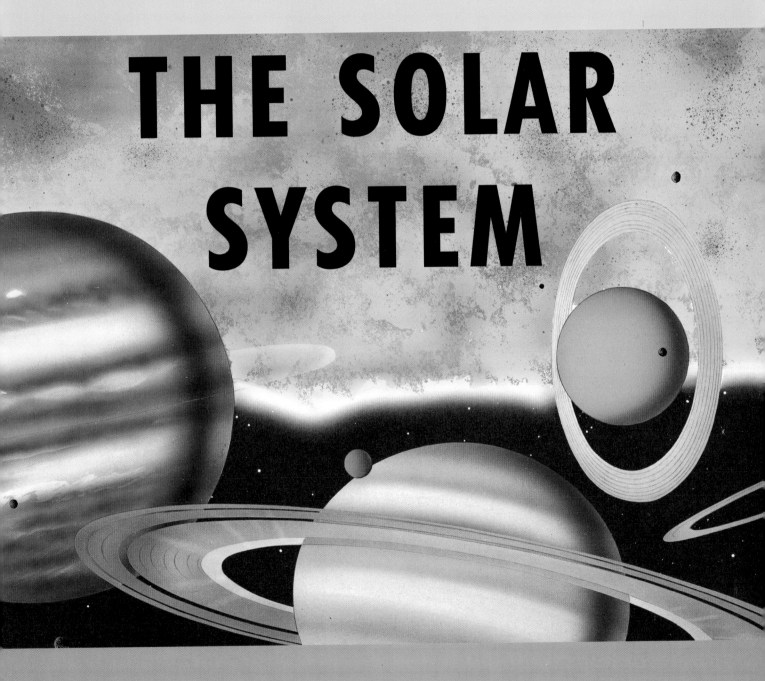

McRae Books

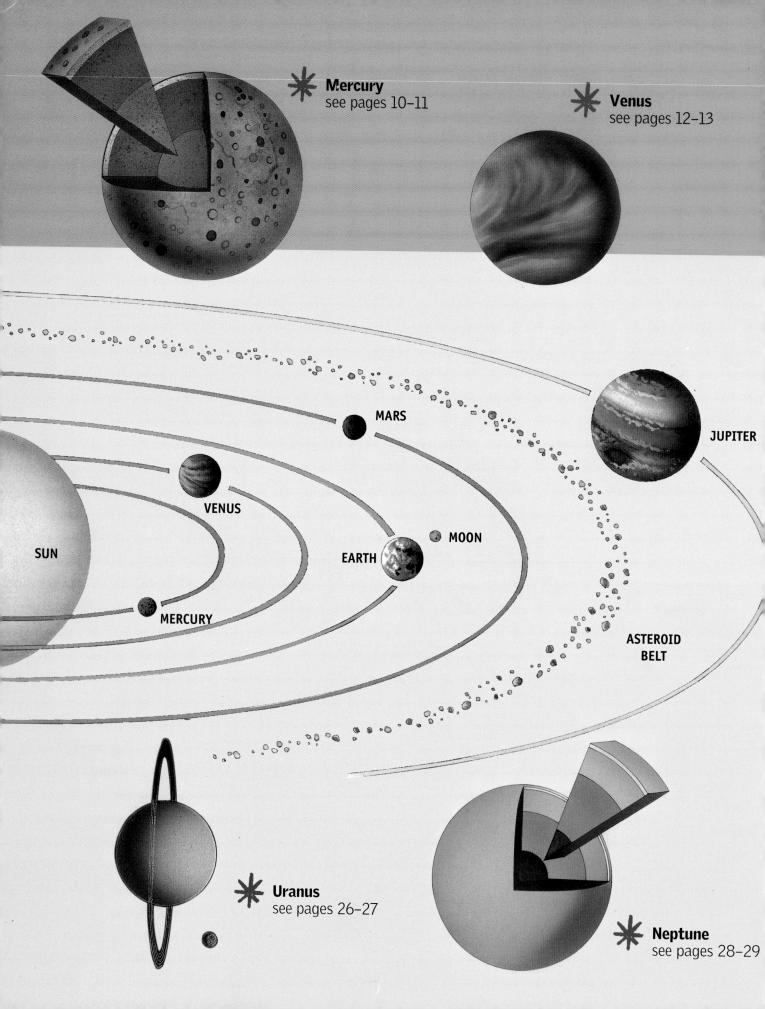

Mercury
see pages 10–11

Venus
see pages 12–13

MARS

JUPITER

VENUS

SUN

MOON

EARTH

MERCURY

ASTEROID
BELT

Uranus
see pages 26–27

Neptune
see pages 28–29

Saturn
see pages 22–23

Comets and
Asteroids
see page 18–19

Contents

Satellites
and Probes
see pages 24–25

Mars
see pages 16–17

The four inner planets—Mercury, Venus, Earth, and Mars—are balls of rock. Venus is the hottest planet, though Mercury is closer to the Sun. Earth looks blue from space, because of the oceans that cover much of its surface.

Mercury

The Sun

Our Sun is just one of billions of stars in the Universe. It is much more massive than any other body in the Solar System. Its gravity holds the planets in their orbits around it. The Sun's light and warmth makes life possible on Earth.

Jupiter and the other three outer planets—Saturn, Uranus, and Neptune —are "gas giants", mainly made of liquid gas and ice. They are much bigger than the inner planets. Jupiter is the biggest planet in the Solar System.

Venus

6

Earth

Jupiter

Mars

Let's Look at the
Solar System

The Solar System is a whirling mass of matter in space, orbiting (revolving around) our star, the Sun. The largest objects in the Solar System are the eight planets. There are also small, dwarf planets, more than a hundred satellites or moons, and many thousands of asteroids, comets, and meteoroids. The space in between is filled with interplanetary dust. The Solar System was formed some 5 billion years ago.

Planets

The eight major planets are: Mercury, Venus, Earth, Mars, Jupiter, Saturn, Uranus, and Neptune. Astronomers counted tiny Pluto as a ninth planet until 2006, when they decided it was really only a dwarf planet. There are several other dwarf planets in the Solar System, and probably more waiting to be discovered.

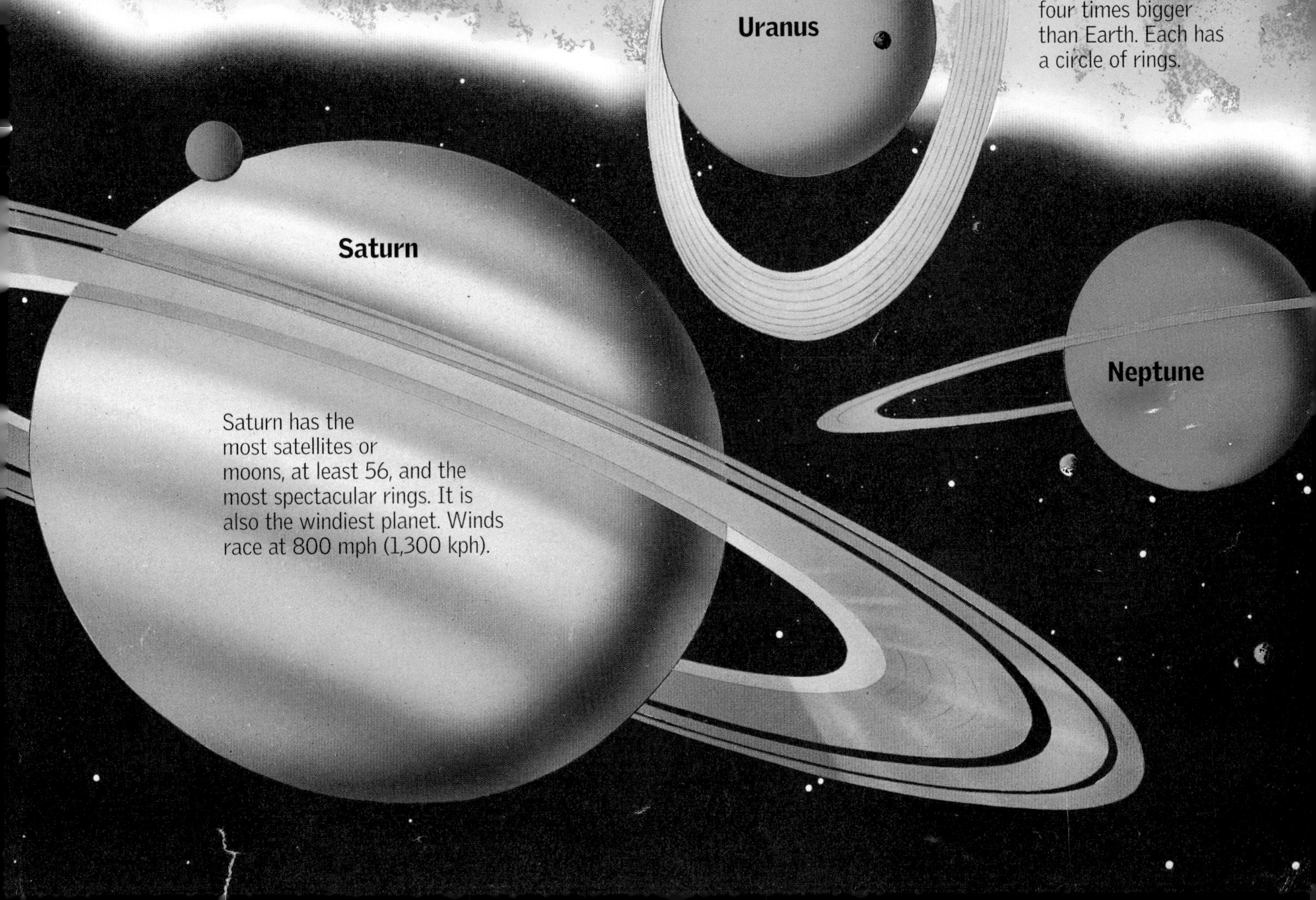

Blue-green Uranus and blue Neptune are four times bigger than Earth. Each has a circle of rings.

Uranus

Saturn

Saturn has the most satellites or moons, at least 56, and the most spectacular rings. It is also the windiest planet. Winds race at 800 mph (1,300 kph).

Neptune

Blue giants explode as supernovas. Red giants shrink, and become tiny white dwarfs.

As they age, some stars expand. They become red or blue giants.

Our Sun is an orange-yellow star in the middle of its life.

Stars are born inside clouds of dust and gas called nebulas.

8

Types of star

RED SUPERGIANT

WHITE DWARF

RED GIANT

YELLOW DWARF

The Sun is a yellow dwarf star. Bigger, brighter stars are giants and supergiants. Blue giants are very bright. White dwarfs are small stars, but incredibly dense.

During its lifetime, a star may expand rapidly and then explode.

The Sun

Like all stars, the Sun is a very dense mass of gas. It is incredibly hot, a nuclear furnace inside which hydrogen atoms are turned into helium. Energy from the Sun radiates out across the Solar System. Light from the Sun takes 8 minutes and 20 seconds to reach Earth, traveling through space at 186,000 miles a second (300,000 km a second).

Lifetime of a star

Stars' lifetimes last billions of years. As they begin to die, they become giants and supergiants, which eventually explode and become white dwarfs.

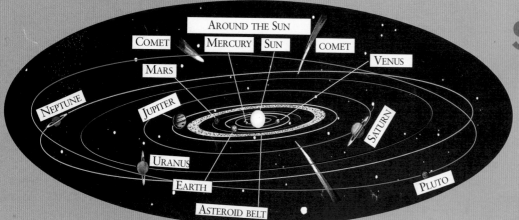

AROUND THE SUN

COMET · MERCURY · SUN · COMET

MARS · VENUS

NEPTUNE · JUPITER · SATURN

URANUS

EARTH · PLUTO

ASTEROID BELT

Solar system

The planets orbit (move around) the Sun at different distances. Mercury is closest to the Sun, and takes just 88 Earth-days for one orbit. Earth takes 365 days—a year. Tiny and far-away Pluto takes 248 years!

Solar eclipse

A solar eclipse happens when the Moon blocks light from the Sun, throwing a shadow on the Earth. In a partial eclipse, the Moon only partly covers the Sun. In a total eclipse, the Moon blots out the Sun for about 7 minutes.

MOON'S ORBIT
EARTH
SUN
MOON

In a total eclipse, the Moon's shadow on the Earth is about 100 miles (140 km) wide.

Size and temperature

The Sun's diameter is 864,000 miles (1,390,435 km). Compare this with Earth, just 7,296 miles (12,756 km). The surface temperature of the Sun is 11,000°F (6,000°C). The center of the Sun reaches 27 million°F (15 million°C).

Close-up of the Sun, showing surface features (a solar flare and Sun spots) and internal workings.

Sun spots

Blotches on the Sun's surface are called Sun spots. They are made by changes in the Sun's magnetic field, and occur over an 11-year cycle.

Sun flares

Solar flares are bright loops of hot gas that emerge from the sunspot regions of the Sun. Huge clouds of glowing gas (called prominences) erupt, driven by magnetic forces to lift off from the Sun. They can span 100,000s of miles over the solar surface, with an average length of 125,000 miles (200,000 km).

Mariner 10

The only spacecraft to have flown close to Mercury so far is Mariner 10, in 1974 and 1975. The probe took the first close-up photographs of the cratered surface, but it was only able to map about half the planet, because the rest was in shadow.

At its closest, Mariner 10 came within about 203 miles (327 km) of Mercury's surface.

The Messenger spacecraft will see the side of Mercury that Mariner 10 was unable to see. It will map the whole planet in color.

Craters

Meteorites that hit the surface of Mercury over four billion years ago left it dotted with craters. Mariner 10 was able to photograph a huge crater named Caloris, the biggest feature so far known on Mercury.

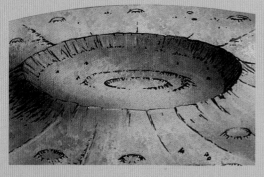

The huge Caloris crater on Mercury.

Messenger

In 2004, the Messenger space probe was launched from Earth on a mission to orbit Mercury. It will reach the planet in 2011. Two of its aims are to measure and record what the planet's surface rocks are made of and how old they are.

Size and speed

Mercury is the second-smallest planet, with a diameter of 3,031 miles (4,878 km). It moves faster than any other planet in the Solar System, at 107,000 mph (172,000 kph). When the Romans saw it 2,000 years ago, they named it Mercury, after the gods' winged messenger.

Mercury (left) and Earth (right) size comparison. Earth is not a big planet, but it is a giant beside Mercury.

Mercury

From Earth, Mercury is hard to see without a telescope, because it is so small and so near the Sun. It is only slightly larger than our Moon, and looks rather like the Moon, with a surface pitted with craters made by meteorites. It is airless, and very hot by day, up to 800°F (430°C). At night, temperatures plunge to a freezing -290°F (-180°C). Mercury has such a thin atmosphere of gases that the sky looks black all the time.

Surface and core

Mercury's surface is probably dusty, like the Moon's, and has some plains and cliffs, and lots of craters. It has a solid core, probably composed of iron, nickel, and other elements.

Sun's distance

Mercury is the nearest planet to the Sun, and takes just 88 Earth days to complete an orbit. On average it is 36 million miles (58 million km) from the Sun. At times, it comes within 28.6 million miles (46 million km).

Even though Mercury is so hot, some of its crater floors never get sunlight and may contain ice.

A cut-away showing Mercury's solid core. The craters were made by meteorites and comets hitting the planet.

Evening star

Venus can be seen from Earth as a bright point of light near the Sun in the western sky. People call it the 'evening star,' because for part of the year it is the first "star" visible as the Sun sets.

Surface and core

Venus has a rocky surface and a crust similar in thickness to Earth's. A thick layer of rock surrounds a core of, probably, semi-molten nickel and iron.

A cut-away showing Venus's core (slightly larger than Earth's.)

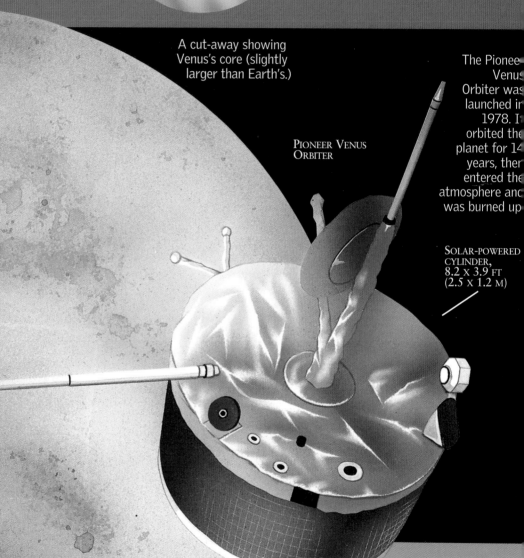

PIONEER VENUS ORBITER

The Pioneer Venus Orbiter was launched in 1978. It orbited the planet for 14 years, then entered the atmosphere and was burned up.

SOLAR-POWERED CYLINDER, 8.2 x 3.9 FT (2.5 x 1.2 M)

Probes

The first spacecraft to observe Venus was Mariner 2 (1962). The Russians were the first to land a probe, Venera 7 (1970); and Venera 9 (1975) took close-up photographs of the surface. Venus Express orbited Venus in 2005–06.

Under pressure

Spacecraft trying to land on Venus have a tough time. Between 1970 and 1986, ten Russian Venera robot probes dropped onto the surface. They all stopped sending back signals after less than an hour. The atmospheric pressure is like being 3,280 ft (1,000 m) deep under our ocean. Any craft that lands on Venus is soon crushed.

Venus's clouds blot out both the Sun by day and the stars at night.

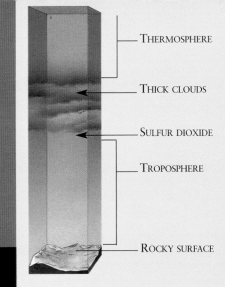

THERMOSPHERE

THICK CLOUDS

SULFUR DIOXIDE

TROPOSPHERE

ROCKY SURFACE

The atmosphere on Venus.

Venus

Venus is only a little smaller than Earth—its diameter is 7,521 miles (12,102 km)—or 95 percent of Earth's. But Venus is much, much hotter than Earth, and is toxic, smoggy, and inhospitable to life. It is hotter even than Mercury, although it is twice as far from the Sun, which is 67.2 million miles (108.2 million km) away. A strange feature of the planet is that it rotates in the opposite direction to Earth.

Heat trap

Venus is wrapped in a very thick atmosphere made up almost entirely of carbon dioxide (96 percent). This prevents heat from escaping, creating a strong greenhouse effect. Temperatures reach over 860°F (460°C).

13

Gases

The main gases in Venus's atmosphere are carbon dioxide, carbon monoxide, nitrogen, argon, neon, and sulfur dioxide. There is water vapor, too, but no water – water would just boil away in the heat.

The Venera 2 probe (1966) passed within 15,000 miles (24,000 km) of Venus.

Volcanoes

The Magellan mission to Venus (1990–1994) revealed that the planet has thousands of volcanoes, many of them huge. But they appear to be inactive. Maat Mons, the tallest volcano, towers 5 miles (8 km) high.

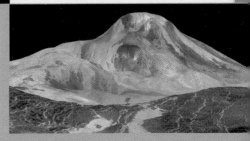
A computer-generated image of Maat Mons. Millions of years ago, the surface of Venus may have been covered in lava.

Earth from spac

The Earth is close enough to the Sun to keep warm, but not so close that i boils or scorches. It has water, and a gaseous atmosphere that protects life on the planet from harmful radiation.

The Earth, seen from space.

14

All Earth's living things depend on th oxygen in the air. Much of this is produced by the trees of the Amazon rain forest.

The Earth's surface temperature varies between about −190°F and 136°F (−88°C and 58°C).

Neil Armstrong, landing on the Moon, famously said: "That's one small step for man one giant leap for mankind."

Earth's core

The Earth has a thin outer crust. This is where life exists. Beneath is a mantle of hot, molten rocks, surrounding two cores—an outer core of melted iron and other elements, and an inner core of iron, with maybe other elements, squeezed under enormous pressure.

CRUST

MANTLE

OUTER CORE

INNER CORE

A cut-away of the Earth, showing the land, oceans, and core.

The Earth

Scientists believe that the Earth began as a cloud of gas and dust swirling in space around the Sun, which at the time was a young star. Earth looks round, but is not a perfect globe—it bulges around the middle, the equator, and the poles are flattened. The Earth supports an amazing richness of life—the only planet in the Solar System that does, so far as we know. It has one large natural satellite, the Moon.

SATELLITE

AURORA

SHUTTLE ORBITER

METEOR

STRATOSPHERE BALLOON

CLOUDS AND AIRCRAFT

SEA LEVEL

Earth's atmosphere is full of activity.

Atmosphere

Surrounding the planet are the layers of the atmosphere, composed mainly of the gases nitrogen (78 percent) and oxygen (21 percent).

Moon landing

The Moon is the Earth's only natural satellite. In 1969, Neil Armstrong of the Apollo 11 mission became the first person to step onto the Moon, having flown 239,000 miles (384,000 km) through space.

A cut-away of the Moon, showing its cratered surface and solid core.

The Moon's structure

The Moon's surface is dry and dusty. The outer crust is rich in aluminum and calcium. Beneath this is a layer of solid rock, then partly melted rock. The central core is made of iron and sulfur.

RO111519461

Landing on Mars

The Mars Pathfinder, carrying the Sojourner rover on board, took off from the USA on December 4, 1996. On July 4, 1997, it entered the Martian atmosphere and came down by parachute, landing on airbags. It then released Sojourner onto the planet.

1. At 5.8 miles (9.3 km) from the surface, Pathfinder's parachute opens.

2. The heatshield is separated and drops away.

3. The lander is lowered. The radar altimeter is activated at 1 mile (1.6 km) from the surface.

4. Airbags inflate 10 seconds before landing. Braking rockets begin at six seconds.

5. Pathfinder has a bumpy landing, using airbags.

Dust storms

Mars is a rock-strewn, dry world that looks like a red sand desert. Powerful winds whip up the dirt into vast dust storms that can cover the planet. Because the atmosphere is so thin, the planet's reddish color can be seen from Earth.

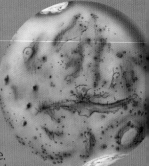

View of the "red planet" from space. The polar ice caps contain water ice.

The Sojourner rover weighed just 23 lb (10.4 kg), and explored about 2,690 sq ft (250 sq m) of Mars' rocky surface.

EACH WHEEL CAN MOVE UP AND DOWN INDEPENDENTLY OF THE OTHERS

ALUMINUM WHEEL WITH CLEATS. SIX WHEELS PROVIDE GREATER STABILITY THAN FOUR.

SOLAR PANEL PROVIDES POWER TO RUN THE ROVER

NASA

FRONT ROCKER-BOGIE

Exploring

Sojourner was the first rover to explore another planet. Using cameras and scientific instruments, it spent 83 days analyzing Martian rocks and soil and sending photographs of the surface back to Earth. Then the flight team lost communication with it.

Mars Pathfinder on Mars' rocky surface.

Surface and core

The surface of Mars is barren and rocky and almost entirely covered in fine red dust. The planet probably has a solid iron-compound core. The core is deep within a molten rock mantle, covered by a thin crust.

A cross section of Mars, showing the cratered surface and solid core. Mars rotates once every 24 hours, like Earth, but it takes almost twice as long to orbit the Sun – 687 days.

Mars

Mars is known as the "red planet." It looks rusty red because its rocks contain iron dust that has oxidised (gone rusty) in the thin atmosphere. A day on Mars is only 40 minutes longer than a day on Earth, and Mars has winters and summers, just as Earth does. But it is much colder and drier than Earth, with temperatures falling to -193°F (-125ºC). Mars is a lot farther than the Earth is from the Sun: 142 million mi (228 million km), compared with Earth's 93 million mi (150 million km).

Moons of Mars

Mars has two small moons, Deimos and Phobos. Even seen through the most powerful telescopes on Earth, they look like minute dots of light. Closer inspection from flyby spacecraft revealed dark, potato-shaped rocky moons. Phobos is covered in grooves and both moons have craters. Phobos travels around Mars in just 7.6 hours; Deimos takes 30.2 hours.

DEIMOS

Olympus Mons

Olympus Mons is the highest point on Mars, and the biggest volcano in the Solar System. It rises 16 miles (26 km) high—three times higher than Earth's Mt Everest. Another feature on Mars is a great chasm, Valles Marineris, which is 2,500 miles (4,000 km) long—long enough to stretch from California to New York.

Olympus Mons (in red) compared with Earth's Mount Everest (in white).

MARS

PHOBOS

Shooting stars that flash across the night sky are actually meteors (lumps of rock or metallic debris) flaring up briefly as they enter Earth's atmosphere. They are visible for only a second or two before they burn up or hit the Earth.

Shooting stars are visible on most dark nights.

Asteroid belt

18

In the main asteroid belt, there are probably millions of asteroids scattered across space. Most are very small, but the biggest (more than 200 identified) are larger than 63 miles (100 km) across. The largest asteroid is Ceres, a rock about 578 mi (930 km) across. Any spacecraft passing through the belt risks a collision.

The main asteroid belt lies between the orbits of Mars and Jupiter.

Comets
and Asteroids

A comet is a chunk of ice, dust, and rock. Comets move around the Sun, but journey far out toward the fringes of the Solar System. Some comets take thousands of years to complete one orbit. Asteroids are mini-planets, though most look like huge, irregular lumps of rock. They orbit the Sun between Mars and Jupiter. Millions of smaller lumps of rock or metal, called meteoroids, also orbit the Sun.

JUPITER

VENUS

MOON

EARTH

MERCURY

ASTEROID BELT

Asteroid origins

Asteroids may be leftover debris from when the Solar System formed, or the remains of an exploded planet that once orbited in the gap between Mars and Jupiter.

Collision course

An asteroid hitting Earth 65 million years ago may have made such an impact, involving dramatic climate change, that it led to the extinction of the dinosaurs. Should a big asteroid be detected on a collision course with Earth in the future, the only remedy would be to send spacecraft to blow it up or push it onto a new course.

In 2005, a spacecraft called Deep Impact was sent into space to blow up part of a comet called Temple 1.

As a comet gets nearer to the Sun, the ice in its core begins to melt, releasing dust and gas in a cloud. Blown by solar wind, the cloud forms a tail streaming out behind the comet.

Brightest comets

Over the last 2,000 years, bright comets visible to the naked eye have occurred only about 5 times per century. Comet Hyakutake (1996) and Comet Hale-Bopp (1997) were both extremely bright. The spectacular bluish-green Hyakutake came closer to the Earth than most comets in the last 200 years, and had the longest tail ever known.

Death of a comet

In July 1994, comet Shoemaker-Levy 9 plunged into Jupiter. This was an event of great interest to scientists, who observed the comet's orbit failing as it was hauled in by Jupiter's massive gravitational force. The comet was shattered into 21 lumps, which crashed into the gas-giant planet itself. The impact sites of the fragments could be seen months after the comet hit Jupiter.

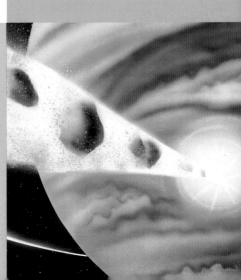

Jupiter is hit by fragments of comet Shoemaker-Levy 9.

A cut-away of Jupiter showing its solid core and liquid layers.

Ring system

Jupiter has rings, like the other gas-giant Saturn. The rings are much fainter, and were first spotted by the Voyager 1 space probe, which visited the planet in 1979. The rings are made of small dust particles.

Jupiter

GANYMEDE

Jupiter is the biggest planet in the Solar System. A giant ball of gas and liquid, it has a diameter of 88,860 miles (143,000 km)—11 times bigger than Earth's. In fact, Jupiter is so big that a thousand Earth-sized planets would fit inside it. It is the fifth planet from the Sun, orbiting at an average distance of 483 million miles (778 million km). Jupiter is named for the king of the Roman gods.

20

Structure

Beneath Jupiter's stormy atmosphere is a planet made of hydrogen and helium, the two lightest gases. It may have a rock core, within a mantle of metallic hydrogen.

The great red spot

The surface of Jupiter is a mass of stormy weather. The biggest storm is the Great Red Spot, a hurricane vortex bigger than our Earth.

Visits to Jupiter

The two Pioneer probes flew close to Jupiter in the 1970s, but Voyagers 1 and 2 (1979) sent back the first clear pictures of Jupiter. Ulysses flew past Jupiter in 1992, and in 1995 Galileo orbited the planet.

The Great Red Spot raging above Jupiter.

Moons of Jupiter

Jupiter has 63 known moons. The four largest are Ganymede, Callisto, Io, and Europa. Ganymede is larger than the planet Mercury, and Europa is unusual because its icy surface is incredibly smooth. Callisto, in contrast, is covered with craters.

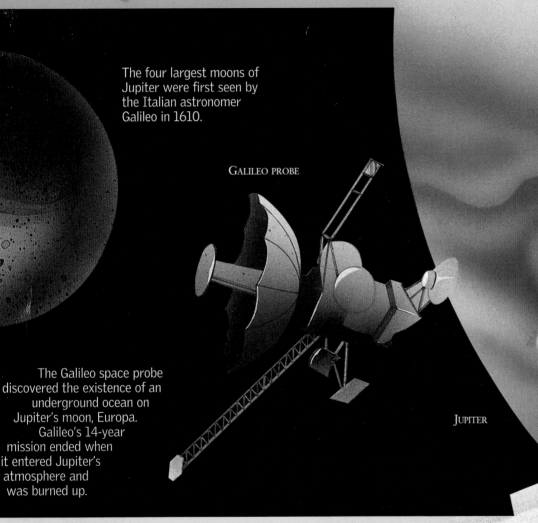

The four largest moons of Jupiter were first seen by the Italian astronomer Galileo in 1610.

GALILEO PROBE

The Galileo space probe discovered the existence of an underground ocean on Jupiter's moon, Europa. Galileo's 14-year mission ended when it entered Jupiter's atmosphere and was burned up.

Io

JUPITER

Volcanoes on Io

Io is the third biggest of Jupiter's moons, and the most volcanically active body in the Solar System; it has nine active volcanoes. It also has rocky "tides" 300 feet (100 m) high, dragged by Jupiter's massive gravity.

Io is covered in sulfur, which gets blasted by volcanoes 200 miles (320 km) into space.

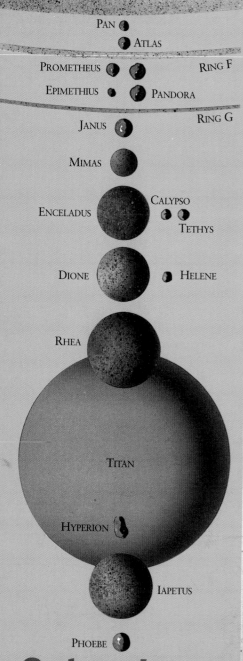

SATURN

PAN

ATLAS

PROMETHEUS

RING F

EPIMETHIUS

PANDORA

JANUS

RING G

MIMAS

ENCELADUS

CALYPSO

TETHYS

DIONE

HELENE

RHEA

TITAN

HYPERION

IAPETUS

PHOEBE

Saturn's moons

Saturn has more moons than any other planet – at least 50. They come in all shapes and sizes; some are rocky, others icy, and some are billions of years old. The largest, Titan, is bigger than the planet Mercury and is the only moon in the Solar System to have a thick atmosphere like Earth's.

Probing Saturn

In their "flybys" of Saturn, the two probes Voyager 1 (in 1980) and Voyager 2 (1981) discovered over 1,000 ringlets and 7 satellites. The Cassini probe, in orbit around Saturn from 2004 to 2008, has extensively photographed Saturn and its moons and rings, and collected data on what they are made of.

VOYAGER 2

Saturn

Saturn, the sixth planet from the Sun, is the most recognizable planet because of its spectacular rings. There are seven major rings, composed of hundreds of thousands of "ringlets." The largest gap between the rings is called the Cassini division. Saturn itself is nearly as big as Jupiter— more than 750 Earths would fit inside it. It is the windiest planet, with gases in the atmosphere racing around at up to 800 mph (1,300 kph).

Superlight giant

Despite being almost ten times the size of Earth, and the second-largest planet in the Solar System, Saturn is amazingly light. Made mostly of liquid hydrogen, it is so light it could float in water.

Most of Saturn is a mass of whirling gases. This produces a colorful, banded effect.

Saturn's rings

Saturn's rings can be seen from Earth through a telescope. They are made up mostly of millions of icy crystals and chunks of rock, some as big as a house. Voyager 2 was able to show that the rings are made of the same material as Saturn's moons.

During its four-year mission to Saturn, Cassini will orbit the planet 74 times and fly close to Titan 44 times. It will also make numerous flybys of Saturn's other moons.

Saturn's ring systems stretch over 300,000 miles (480,000 km) out into space, but the rings are less than 140 ft (30 m) thick.

SATURN

ENGINES

CASSINI PROBE

23

MAGNETOMETER BOOM

ANTENNA

RADAR BAY

Shepherd moons

Around eight of Saturn's moons orbit at the edge of rings. Their gravity-pull helps to keep the rings in shape. Scientists call these moons "shepherds."

Hubble

The Hubble Space Telescope (1990) revolutionized star-gazing. Hubble orbits the Earth at about 375 miles (600 km), once every 97 minutes. From space it can see clear images of distant galaxies and nebulae, free of the distortions caused by the Earth's atmosphere.

Hubble is 43.5 feet (12.2 m) long.

SPUTNIK 1

Sputnik 1 (1957) was the first space satellite.

Sputnik 1

The launch of Russia's Sputnik 1, in October 1957, opened the era of modern space exploration. It was followed a month later by Sputnik 2, carrying a dog named Laika into space.

24

Pioneer 11

Space probes send data back to Earth from millions of miles away. This image of Saturn was sent by Pioneer 11. In 1983, Pioneer 11 left the Solar System, 11 years after leaving Earth.

NASA's Pioneer 11 image of Saturn and its moon Titan at the upper left.

Satellites
and probes

An artificial satellite is a spacecraft that orbits a planet. Satellites in Earth orbit are used for communication, weather forecasting, navigation, military surveillance, and scientific research. There are around 2,500 satellites orbiting the Earth. A space probe is a robot spacecraft sent to explore distant planets. Such space voyages take years, and some probes have flown far beyond the edges of the Solar System.

A space probe carrying a camera, a star tracker, and a magnetometer for measuring magnetism.

Space probes

Space probes are solar-powered robots that send back data and pictures by radio to Earth. Some probes are satellites, because they orbit planets. Others are sent to explore deep space and may not orbit planets, so are not technically satellites.
Voyager 2 visited Jupiter (1979), Saturn (1981), Uranus (1986), and Neptune (1989).

Landing on Titan

In 2005, Cassini sent the Huygens probe down onto Saturn's moon Titan. The lander slowed down from over 13,000 mph (21,000 kph) to 895 mph (1,440 kph) in less than two minutes. Huygens' final descent was made by parachute.

HUYGENS PROBE

Many of Uranus's moons are made mostly of ice, not rock.

The methane gas in Uranus's atmosphere absorbs the red light in sunlight, but scatters blue light into space, which is why Uranus looks blue-green.

Voyager 2 is the only spacecraft to have visited Uranus. It passed by on January 24, 1986.

Most of Uranus' moons are named after characters in Shakespeare plays, for example Oberon, Cordelia, Ophelia, and Desdemona.

Surface and core

Uranus is an icy planet. It has layers of cloud, composed mainly of hydrogen, with some helium and methane. Beneath the clouds is a liquid layer of hydrogen and helium, and then a semi-solid layer that may include ammonia. At the core is molten rock.

LAYERED ATMOSPHERE

LIQUID HYDROGEN

SEMI-SOLID LAYER

MOLTEN ROCK CORE

Cut-away of Uranus, showing its atmosphere, layers, and core.

Uranus

Uranus is about four times bigger than Earth and appears blue-green. It has at least 27 moons and 11 rings. A notable feature is that it spins oddly. The interior takes just over 17 hours to rotate once, but most of the atmosphere takes much less time to complete a rotation. Uranus was discovered in 1781 by the astronomer William Herschel. Odd "wobbles" in its orbit suggested it was being affected by the gravitational pull of another planet, and in 1846 astronomers identified Neptune as the cause.

Knocked over

Uranus's sideways tilt may have been caused millions of years ago by a collision with a giant asteroid.

The rings of Uranus were only discovered in 1977.

Miranda

Miranda—one of the moons of Uranus—appears to be a jumbled mass of ice. It looks as if it was once smashed into fragments and then forced back into a ball by gravity.

MIRANDA

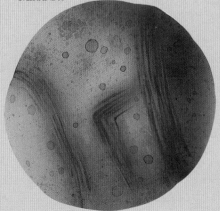

Sideways tilt

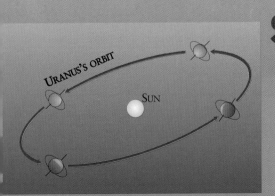

URANUS'S ORBIT

SUN

As it orbits the Sun, Uranus tilts on its axis much more than any other planet. This means that for part of its orbit, the north pole points toward the Sun, and for part of it, it points away, giving each pole a 42-year period of continual sunlight or darkness.

Structure

Like Uranus, Neptune has an atmosphere of hydrogen, helium, and methane gases. At the mantle, these gases are compressed into a slushy mass around a central core, probably made of rock and ice.

OUTER MANTLE

ATMOSPHERE

INNER MANTLE

CORE

Cutaway of Neptune showing its mantle and core.

The high winds that blast Neptune's clouds move at up to 1,300 mph (2,100 kph).

Neptune

Neptune is a far-distant, stormy blue planet, a ball of gas and liquid four times the size of Earth. Like Uranus, it is too distant to be seen without a telescope. It is about 30 times farther away from the Sun than Earth is, and takes 165 Earth-years to make a single orbit of the Sun. Neptune has 13 known moons, the largest of which is Triton. Triton is the only major satellite in the Solar System that orbits its planet "the wrong way," in the opposite direction to the planet itself.

Neptune's clouds

Neptune's high clouds are made of methane gas. They are blown by the strongest planetary winds in the Solar System, at over 700 mph (1,125 kph). Darker clouds lower in the atmosphere may be made of hydrogen sulfide.

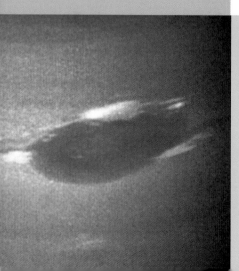

Neptune's great dark spot

The Voyager 2 spacecraft discovered a hurricane-like gas storm on Neptune, similar to Jupiter's Great Red Spot. Scientists named it the Great Dark Spot. By 1994, however, the storm had ended, and the Spot was gone.

The Great Dark Spot.

Rings

Neptune's outer ring is unusual in having sections that are brighter than the rest of the ring.

Neptune's rings are less distinct than Saturn's.

Triton

Neptune's largest moon, Triton, measures 1,620 miles (2,700 km) in diameter. The surface is covered in ice, and the poles are capped with pink snow of frozen nitrogen.

Triton's eruptions

Left, a gas-geyser on Triton, with Neptune beyond.

Triton has volcanoes and geysers that blast nitrogen ice crystals and vapor into the atmosphere. With a surface temperature of -390°F (-195°C), it is the coldest known place in the Solar System.

Most of Triton's surface is icy.

VOYAGER 2

Voyager 2

Voyager 2 sent back the first close-ups of Neptune in 1989. It revealed Neptune's rings, and six previously unknown moons.

Comets and asteroids

Comets orbit the Sun in the Kuiper Belt, beyond Pluto, or farther out in the Oort Cloud. Only a few comets pass close to the Sun at regular, fairly short intervals, including Halley's Comet, every 75–76 years.

Pluto and Charon

The "planet" Pluto was discovered in 1930, but in 2006 it was downgraded to the status of dwarf planet. One of its moons, Charon, was discovered in 1978. Two further moons were discovered in 2005.

Pluto and its moon Charon.

The space probes Pioneer 10, Pioneer 11, Voyager 1, and Voyager 2 have all now traveled beyond the most distant planet in the Solar System. They continue on their journeys, as far as we know, into deep space.

Voyager 1 is the most distant human-made object in space. It is over 9.3 billion miles (15 billion km) away.

The very last radio signal from Pioneer 10 was received in 2003.

New discoveries

New dwarf planets are still being discovered orbiting the Sun at the extreme edges of the Solar System. These include Sedna, Quaoar, and Zena. Zena's diameter is only 1,500 miles (2,400 km) across. These dwarf planets orbit in the disk-shaped Kuiper Belt.

Charon is believed to be almost identical in structure to its parent planet, Pluto.

Sedna's position in the Solar System.

SEDNA

SUN

NEPTUNE

PLUTO

The Edges of the Solar System

At the edges of the Solar System, the Sun appears to be just an extra-brilliant star. Little heat reaches this remote realm. Beyond the orbit of Neptune is the Kuiper Belt, containing many small icy bodies and dwarf planets such as Pluto and Sedna. At the very edge of the Solar System is the huge Oort Cloud, containing billions of frozen comets. In 2006, NASA launched a new probe, named New Horizons, which will make a one-way journey to the Kuiper Belt to find out more about Pluto.

Pluto's structure

Pluto is a cold, rocky mass. Scientists estimate that it is 70 percent rock and 30 percent water ice, surrounded by frozen nitrogen, solid methane, and carbon dioxide. The thin atmosphere is likely to contain nitrogen, carbon monoxide, and methane gas.

ATMOSPHERE
MANTLE
CORE

New Horizons probe

The New Horizons space probe was launched in 2006 from Cape Canaveral, Florida, and should reach Pluto in 2015. In February 2007 it flew past Jupiter. The probe is very small, at only 8 ft (2.4 m) wide. It has a nuclear power supply for generating electricity, and seven scientific instruments for studying Pluto and its moons.

Cutaway of Pluto showing its structure. Temperatures on Pluto hover around -396°F (-238°C).

Index